PowerKiDS
Readers
SAFARI ANIMALS

CHEETAHS

Clara Reade

PowerKiDS
press

New York

For Matthew Sawyer Tu

Published in 2013 by The Rosen Publishing Group, Inc.
29 East 21st Street, New York, NY 10010

First Edition

Editor: Amelie von Zumbusch
Book Design: Greg Tucker

Photo Credits: Cover, pp. 5, 7, 9, 11, 13, 15, 17, 19, 21, 23, 24 Shutterstock.com.

Library of Congress Cataloging-in-Publication Data

Reade, Clara.
 Cheetahs / by Clara Reade. — 1st ed.
    p. cm. — (Powerkids readers: Safari animals)
 Includes index.
 ISBN 978-1-4488-7464-4 (library binding) — ISBN 978-1-4488-7471-2 (pbk.) — ISBN 978-1-4488-7544-3 (6-pack)
 1. Cheetah—Juvenile literature. I. Title.
 QL737.C23R427 2013
 599.75'9–dc23
                          2011046781

Manufactured in the United States of America

CPSIA Compliance Information: Batch #CS12PK: For Further Information contact Rosen Publishing, New York, New York at 1-800-237-9932

CONTENTS

Cheetahs run fast!

They cannot run for long.

They get tired.

9

Cheetahs live on **plains**.

They live in Africa and Asia.

13

Adults hunt for food.

Antelopes are their main food.

They hunt during the day.

19

Baby cheetahs are **cubs**.

They live with their mothers.

23

WORDS TO KNOW

cheetah

cubs

plains

INDEX

WEBSITES

Due to the changing nature of Internet links, PowerKids Press has developed an online list of websites related to the subject of this book. This site is updated regularly. Please use this link to access the list: www.powerkidslinks.com/pkrs/cheet/